The Wood Design Awards 2003

A NORTH AMERICAN PROGRAM OF ARCHITECTURAL EXCELLENCE

Tuns Press
Faculty of Architecture and Planning
Dalhousie University
P.O. Box 1000
Halifax, Nova Scotia
Canada B3J 2X4
tunspress.dal.ca

The Wood Design Awards 2003

Editor: Don Griffith, Janam Publications Inc.
Design: Marie-Noëlle Massé, Janam Publications Inc.
Production: Donald Westin
Printing: Friesens

National Library of Canada Cataloguing in Publication

Wood Design Awards 2003 / edited by Don Griffith.

ISSN 1708-5233 The Wood Design Awards
ISBN 0-929112-50-4 (2003)

1. Building, Wooden–Canada.
2. Building, Wooden–United States.
3. Architecture–Awards–Canada.
4. Architecture–Awards–United States.
5. Architecture–Canada–21st century.
6. Architecture–United States–21st century.
I. Griffith, Don

NA4110.W66 2003   721'.0448'097109051   C2003-905316-4

Cover: Maison Goulet, Saia Barbarese Topouzanov architectes   Photo: Marc Cramer

The Wood Design Awards 2003

A NORTH AMERICAN PROGRAM OF ARCHITECTURAL EXCELLENCE

The Wood Design Awards is the only North American Program to recognize and award excellence in wood architecture, and thus to publicly acknowledge the importance of architecture to our society.

The annual Program is open to new and remodeled residential and non-residential projects and building interiors from the U.S. and Canada. Awarded projects push the conventional boundaries of wood as a construction and finishing material.

The 13 awarded projects of 2003 are fully described in this book, and were selected from 217 submissions. They reveal some of the best architectural design occurring in the U.S. and Canada today in the building scales most commonly found in our towns and cities. This book serves as a lasting reference of construction ideas and design inspiration.

The Wood Design Awards is offered by Wood Design & Building and Wood Le Bois magazines [www.woodmags.com], and managed by Janam Publications Inc. We gratefully acknowledge the support of our sponsors and supporting associations: Structurlam Products Inc., Arch Wood Protection/Dricon, Open Joist 2000, The Hardwood Council, The Western Red Cedar Lumber Association, the Canadian Wood Council, and the Sustainable Forestry Initiative, [SFI], a program of the American Forest & Paper Association.

Don Griffith
Coordinator, The Wood Design Awards

WOOD DESIGN BUILDING
WOOD LE BOIS
The Wood Design Awards

2003 Sponsors

STRUCTURLAM
INNOVATIVE GLULAM SPECIALISTS
www.structurlam.com

DRICON
Fire Retardant Treated Wood
www.dricon.com

OPEN JOIST 2000
www.openjoist2000.com

Supporting Associations

Canadian Wood Council Conseil canadien du bois
www.cwc.ca

SUSTAINABLE FORESTRY INITIATIVE
www.aboutsfi.org

REALCEDAR
www.realcedar.org

The Hardwood Council
www.hardwoodcouncil.com

The 2003 Jury

Peter Bohlin is a founding principal of Bohlin Cywinski Jackson, established in 1965. The firm's work is known for exceptional design that is commited to the particularity of place and user. Some recent projects include the Seattle City Hall, Liberty Bell Center, and the Catholic University Student Center. The firm has received more than 200 regional, national and international awards. In 1994, it received the Architecture Firm Award from the American Institute of Architects. *www.bcj.com*

Raymond Moriyama co-founded Moriyama & Teshima Architects in 1958, a firm that has completed prestigious projects, including the Canadian Embassy in Tokyo, the Toronto Reference Library, the Saudi Arabian National Museum in Riyadh, and the new Canadian War Museum. Moriyama has received honorary degrees from nine Canadian universities, Officer of the Order of Canada, the Royal Architectural Institute of Canada Gold Medal, Fellow of the Royal Architectural Institute of Canada, Honorary Fellow of the American Institute of Architects, and Fellow of the Royal Society of the Arts [U.K.]. *www.mtarch.com*

Laura Hartman has helped establish the reputation of Fernau & Hartman Architects as a firm known for diversity and excellence. It has received many awards for architectural design, interior design and technical innovation. Notable projects include: the Napa Valley Museum in Yountville, CA, the Oxygen Media Headquarters in New York, and numerous houses. She has taught at Berkeley, and was the Pietro Belluschi Professor at the University of Oregon in 1998. Hartman has been a member of the Wood Design & Building editorial board since 1998. *www.fernauhartman.com*

We thank our jurors for the diligence and care in selecting the 13 projects of the 2003 Program from a total of 217 submissions.

Peter Bohlin, FAIA,
Principal
Bohlin Cywinski Jackson
Wilkes-Barre, Pittsburgh, Philadelphia,
Seattle and Berkeley [left]

Raymond Moriyama,
FRAIC, Hon. FAIA,
Principal
Moriyama & Teshima Architects
Toronto, Ontario [center]

Laura Hartman,
Principal
Fernau & Hartman Architects, Inc.
Berkeley, California [right]

[Photo: Roy Grogan]

Table of Contents

Honor Awards

Minneapolis Rowing Club

VJAA (VINCENT JAMES ASSOCIATES ARCHITECTS)

The Minneapolis Rowing Club replaces one destroyed by fire. It is a private, nonprofit organization that operates on membership fees and volunteer support.

The building sits above the flood plain of the Mississippi River, 90ft. below the Lake Street Bridge and halfway between Minneapolis and St. Paul. Zoning restrictions set the maximum building height at 35ft., and confine buildings to a long, narrow area where a second boathouse will also be constructed.

The building program consists of 5,500sf for boat storage and 3,000sf for training, locker rooms and meeting space. In an attempt to capture the power, grace and rhythm of the sport, the form of the building draws on an oar's inspiration from the movement of an oar through water.

Other design considerations included: use of common, inexpensive materials, involvement of club members in the construction process, facilitating boat storage, movement and maintenance, and providing structures resistant to vandalism on the isolated site.

The windowless ground floor accommodates the storage racks for the club's rowing sculls. The continuity of the black-painted shiplap siding is interrupted only by copper-clad sliding access doors and corner reveals. Bands of clerestory polycarbonate glazing expand to story height at the upturned corners of the roof. Behind the glazing, mezzanine galleries house exercise areas that have sweeping views of the Mississippi River.

Internally, the careful manipulation and repetition of the slender, highly articulated structure recalls both the rhythmic quality of rowing and the finely crafted shells that one associates with the sport. The mezzanines, their supporting columns lost to view amid the stacked boat hulls, appear to float within the space. The building is uninsulated and the structure laid bare resulting in a powerful, skeletal quality.

The roof curve has the wave-like structure of a hyperbolic paraboloid generated by the incremental rotation of the inverted glulam and steel cable trusses around a neutral axis along the length of the building.

Longitudinal shear resistance is provided by diagonal bracing between the trusses at intervals along the building. The majority of lateral stability, however, comes from the mezzanine floor structures, which are tied into the perimeter walls and supported on glulam columns.

Perimeter columns are secured to a grade beam by concealed steel plates designed as pin connections. Despite its visual complexity, the structure is extremely economic in its use of materials, and in its repetition of a small number of simple details.

Jury – Inventiveness, simplicity and a joyful economy of means have been combined to make an extraordinary building. The repetitive nature of exposed wood framing communicates a clear building solution that has a wonderful quality of space and light.

East elevation

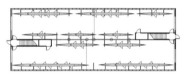

First floor

Second floor

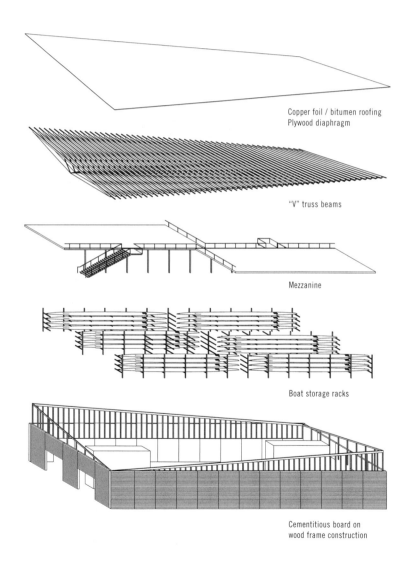

Copper foil / bitumen roofing
Plywood diaphragm

"V" truss beams

Mezzanine

Boat storage racks

Cementitious board on
wood frame construction

Product Specs

Frame
– Glulam wall columns, 3-1/8 x 9, glulam truss chords, 3-1/8 x 12, plywood wall sheathing, glulam suppied by Western Archrib, Boissevain, Manitoba

Exterior
– Modified bitumen roof 2.4 mm, Siplast Veral copper roof system 3.5mm, plywood roof diaphragm 3/4-in., two layers; Polygal polycarbonate glazing, 16mm; Hardiplank fiber-cement lap siding by James Hardie, 5/16-in. thick, 3in. exposed

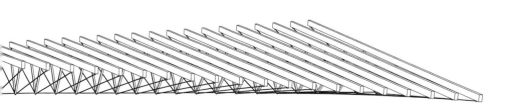

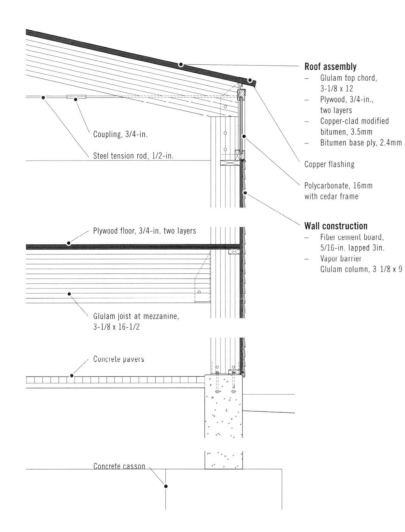

Roof assembly
- Glulam top chord, 3-1/8 x 12
- Plywood, 3/4-in., two layers
- Copper-clad modified bitumen, 3.5mm
- Bitumen base ply, 2.4mm

Copper flashing

Polycarbonate, 16mm with cedar frame

Wall construction
- Fiber cement board, 5/16-in. lapped 3in.
- Vapor barrier Glulam column, 3 1/8 x 9

Coupling, 3/4-in.

Steel tension rod, 1/2-in.

Plywood floor, 3/4-in. two layers

Glulam joist at mezzanine, 3-1/8 x 16-1/2

Concrete pavers

Concrete casson

Section, truss to column connection

Each glulam top chord is identical, and the steel plate that connects it to the perimeter column is designed to accommodate the variations in connection geometry. As a result, the only custom cutting required was to the top of each column.

CLIENT
Minneapolis Rowing Club,
Minneapolis, Minnesota

ARCHITECT
VJAA [Vincent James Associates
Architects], Minneapolis, Minnesota

STRUCTURAL ENGINEER
Bruno Franck, Carroll + Franck Associates,
St. Paul, Minnesota

GENERAL CONTRACTOR
Flannery Construction,
St. Paul, Minnesota

PHOTOS
Mary Ludington, Minneapolis, Minnesota

second wall. The second wall extends full height to the level of the uppermost top plate, making a spine for the sculpted volume of the large living room.

In fair weather, the large doors of the ground-level screened loggias open, extending the interior spaces to the exterior. On the second floor, openings under the gables create infinite perspectives to the outside, a provision that serves to reinforce the initial parti while orienting users to their position in the landscape.

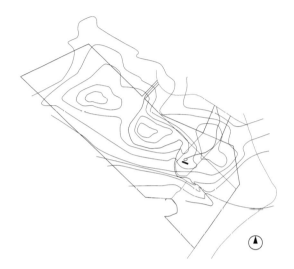

Natural indigenous materials are fundamental to the project. Wood construction recalls the traditional building of the Quebec countryside but is used as a contemporary expression of this heritage. An exposed Douglas fir plywood skin over insulated wood framing provides intimacy and a united composition to the interior. The use of full-size sheets lends a purity to the design, not through elaboration but by sculpting them volumetrically in which simple openings and folds have articulate expression. Hardwood is found in the custom white oak windows and doors, and in the yellow birch flooring of the second level.

The architecture is linked to the topography of the site, the climate, the sun, and the mosquitoes. It is a house that offers numerous escapes, not least from the realms of nostalgia and convention.

Jury – The project has a very legible plan resulting in a powerful building with the additional attribute of using everyday materials. The monolithic use of full panels of Douglas fir plywood creates an exciting, yet refined interior.

Second floor

Ground floor

Product Specs

Frame
— Balloon wood-frame construction, steel reinforced; metal-plate connected wood scissor trusses and plywood 5/8-in. sheathing

Exterior
— Zinc panels [VM ZINC distributed by Canadian Brass and Copper Co.] on plywood sheathing

Interior
— Douglas fir plywood for walls and ceilings; ground floor finished with sawn stone, second floor with oiled yellow birch, water-based varnish [MICCA]; Douglas fir for soffits and ceilings of loggias

Windows/doors
— Custom made in white oak by E. Paquin Inc., Piedmont, Quebec

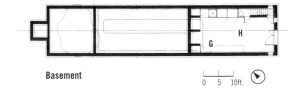

Basement

0 5 10ft.

A   Office
B   Bedroom
C   Master bedroom
D   Terrace
E   Living room
F   Kitchen
G   Studio
H   Storage

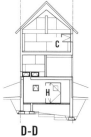

A-A   B-B   C-C   D-D

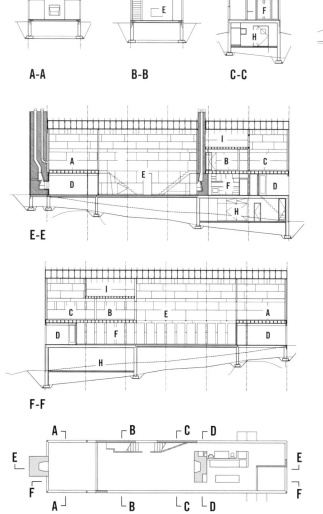

E-E

F-F

A   Office
B   Bedroom
C   Master bedroom
D   Terrace
E   Living room
F   Kitchen
G   Studio
H   Storage
I   Loft

Sections

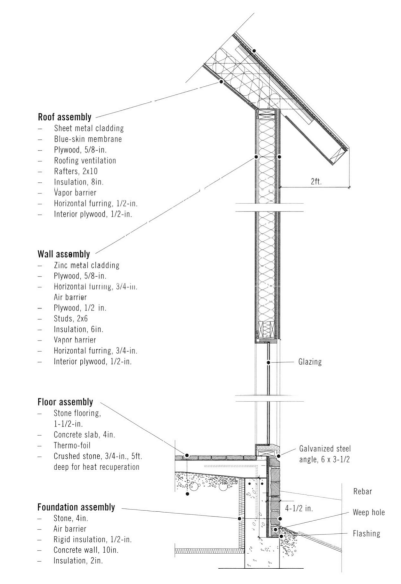

Roof assembly
- Sheet metal cladding
- Blue-skin membrane
- Plywood, 5/8-in.
- Roofing ventilation
- Rafters, 2x10
- Insulation, 8in.
- Vapor barrier
- Horizontal furring, 1/2-in.
- Interior plywood, 1/2-in.

Wall assembly
- Zinc metal cladding
- Plywood, 5/8-in.
- Horizontal furring, 3/4-in.
- Air barrier
- Plywood, 1/2 in.
- Studs, 2x6
- Insulation, 6in.
- Vapor barrier
- Horizontal furring, 3/4-in.
- Interior plywood, 1/2-in.

Floor assembly
- Stone flooring, 1-1/2-in.
- Concrete slab, 4in.
- Thermo-foil
- Crushed stone, 3/4-in., 5ft. deep for heat recuperation

Foundation assembly
- Stone, 4in.
- Air barrier
- Rigid insulation, 1/2-in.
- Concrete wall, 10in.
- Insulation, 2in.

2ft.

Glazing

Galvanized steel angle, 6 x 3-1/2

Rebar

4-1/2 in.

Weep hole

Flashing

South wall section

CLIENT
Marlène Goulet, Montreal, Quebec

ARCHITECT
Mario Saia, Saia Barbarese
Topouzanov architectes, Montreal, Quebec

STRUCTURAL ENGINEER
Jean Saia, Saia Deslauriers Kadanof
et associés inc., Montreal, Quebec

GENERAL CONTRACTOR
Michel Riopel, Construction et Rénovation,
Entrelacs, Quebec

PHOTOS
Frédéric Saia and Marc Cramer,
Montreal, Quebec

Merit Awards

Riddell Residence

WILL BRUDER ARCHITECTS, LTD.

The 2,500sf bungalow was conceived as a wooden sculpture, a refined, simply organized pavilion for life, work and leisure on a forested site in Wilson, Wyoming. The home celebrates the needs of a painter and a photographer, and their passion for the outdoors.

Planned from the outside-in and the inside-out, the long, low house is approached on a gently winding drive level with the datum of entry to emphasize the human scale. The simple asymmetrical ridge gable, immediately evident on arrival at the south elevation, re-interprets local building forms.

Standard platform framing incorporates glulam beams at the ridge and eaves, and open web wood trusses as rafters to allow the flexibility of a vaulted ceiling in the living room. Vertical 1x3 resawn cedar left to weather on the gable end walls, and streak-stained by a grid pattern of black iron nails, makes a taut modern skin that has the serenity of a simple Wyoming shed. Polished stainless steel frame windows set flush with the rhythm of the cedar siding accentuate the tautness of the exterior and hint of interior refinement.

Invention and detail is everywhere considered, from the ridge cap of the cedar shingle roof, to the playfully sculptured and placed roof snow cleats, to the metal knife-edge roof drip and end gable fin-walls. Below the precise edge of the soffit line, the walls of the long elevations have sculptured surfaces of flat-lock seam zinc siding, horizontal cedar siding, and flush-detailed glazed openings.

The interior divides between private and public domains. The compressed entry gallery of maple paneling runs diagonally until arriving at the common living-dining-kitchen area where the vertical scale enlarges to a vaulted ceiling, and a wall of glazing frames the aspen grove beyond.

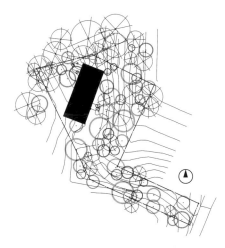

Black slate and maple strip flooring, custom flush maple cabinets with burnished stainless steel counters, and translucent fiberglass sliding shoji screens complement simple off-white gypsum board walls. Maple panel doors conceal the bedrooms, allowing the owners and guests to understand and use the house in a variety of modes.

Jury – The project could be considered a pleasing surprise by taking what superficially seems to be an everyday form and resolving it beautifully with a minimal use of elegant details. Sitting snugly in the forest, the house is comfortably restrained.

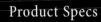

Product Specs

Frame
– Platform frame construction, glulam ridge and eave beams [east eave: 6-3/4 in. x 10-1/2 in.; west eave: 6-3/4 in. x 13-1/2 in.; ridge beam: 6-3/4 in. x 28-1/2 in.] and rafters of Trus Joist metal web wood trusses, 16in. deep at 16in. o.c., 5/8-in. plywood roof sheathing; Trus Joist I-joist floors, 11-7/8 in. deep at 16in. o.c.

Exterior
– Western red cedar shingles, flat-lock seam zinc siding, horizontal cedar siding, vertical 1x3 resawn cedar left to weather, redwood 2x6 outdoor deck

Interior
– Maple plywood wall panels, millwork and cabinets, strip maple flooring, 3/4-in. and slate tile flooring

Windows/doors
– Insulated modular glass with stainless steel frame

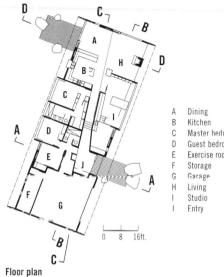

Floor plan

A Dining
B Kitchen
C Master bedroom
D Guest bedroom
E Exercise room
F Storage
G Garage
H Living
I Studio
I Entry

0 8 16ft.

Section A-A

Section B-B

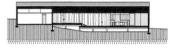

Section C-C

Section D-D

South elevation

East elevation

West elevation

North elevation

CLIENT
The Riddells, Wilson, Wyoming

ARCHITECT
Will Bruder Architects, Ltd.,
Phoenix, Arizona

STRUCTURAL ENGINEER
Rudow & Berry, Scottsdale, Arizona

GENERAL CONTRACTOR
Deon F. Heiner, Continental Construction,
Alpine, Wyoming

PHOTOS
Bill Timmermann, Phoenix, Arizona

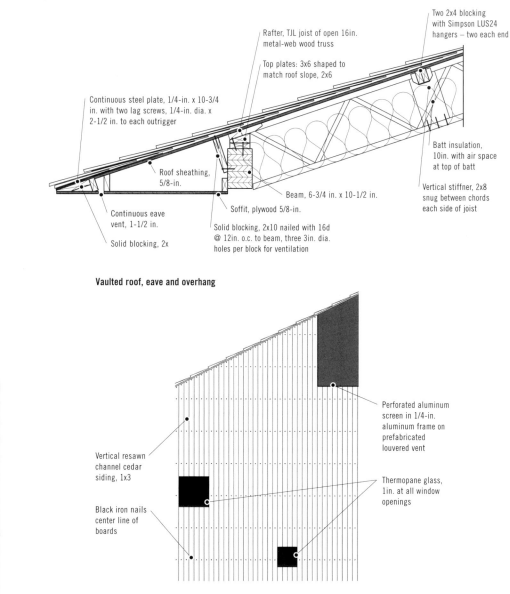

Two 2x4 blocking
with Simpson LUS24
hangers — two each end

Rafter, TJL joist of open 16in.
metal-web wood truss

Top plates: 3x6 shaped to
match roof slope, 2x6

Continuous steel plate, 1/4-in. x 10-3/4
in. with two lag screws, 1/4-in. dia. x
2-1/2 in. to each outrigger

Batt insulation,
10in. with air space
at top of batt

Vertical stiffner, 2x8
snug between chords
each side of joist

Roof sheathing,
5/8-in.

Beam, 6-3/4 in. x 10-1/2 in.

Continuous eave
vent, 1-1/2 in.

Soffit, plywood 5/8-in.

Solid blocking, 2x

Solid blocking, 2x10 nailed with 16d
@ 12in. o.c. to beam, three 3in. dia.
holes per block for ventilation

Vaulted roof, eave and overhang

Perforated aluminum
screen in 1/4-in.
aluminum frame on
prefabricated
louvered vent

Vertical resawn
channel cedar
siding, 1x3

Thermopane glass,
1in. at all window
openings

Black iron nails
center line of
boards

Emerson Sauna

SALMELA ARCHITECT

The outdoor, wood-fired sauna is a unique experience in northern Minnesota. Traditionally, Saturday night was "sauna night" when smoke rose from the sauna chimneys on farmsteads throughout the countryside.

The clients own a semi-secluded site on a lake in northern Minnesota. The formal vocabulary of the sauna contrasts with the architectural language of the client's house nearby. Its use of simple geometric forms, choice of materials and positioning facilitates the steaming, showering and cooling activities of a sauna.

The sauna room tucks into the back of the structure of sod-covered flat roof, in reference to traditional Finnish farmsteads, and red brick that provides heat-holding mass for the interior and a dark, warm ambiance resembling the first saunas that were built partially underground. Smoke from the wood-burning stove vents through a chimney made tall enough to direct smoke above the height of the cooling room.

The cooling process is not formalized in most saunas. However, in the Emerson sauna the cooling area is celebrated in an elevated cooling chamber consisting of a triangular laminated wood tube. The roof of the tube is constructed of screw-laminated 2x4s that interweave at the peak, and of screw-laminated 2x6s for the floor that interweave at the roof-to-floor interface.

Screws of the type found in Structural Insulated Panels were used, having a length of 4-1/2 in. with 3in. of smooth shank and 1-1/2 in. of thread. Each screw fully penetrates three, 2x lumber pieces and partly embeds in the fourth piece. Construction of the triangular frame began on the ground, then was hoisted and braced for construction to continue in place.

The tube cantilevers beyond a supporting curved brick wall that also serves as an open-air shower. The thinness and lightness of the wood construction has an elemental simplicity while the repeating strips of wood inside make one feel secure and uninhibited. The western red cedar lap board roof protects the framing and embodies the notion of horizontal relaxation. Glazed and screened at both ends, and looking south towards the lake and north over the sod roof of the sauna room, the cooling chamber creates a wind channel.

Wood continues into the sauna area in the form of Douglas fir ceilings, doors, benches, and cabinets all blending with the brick, slate, copper and sod roof.

Jury – The project makes skillful use of basic geometric shapes that intersect to make a strong building with textures of wood, brick, glass and sod roof. The prominent gable roof has the intriguing quality of seeming to float above the structure.

Product Specs

Frame
Sauna room of brick cavity wall construction; roof of ceiling joists, sheathing, membrane and sod; cooling chamber of screw-laminated 2x4s that interweave at the peak, and of screw laminated 2x6s for the floor that interweave at the roof-to-floor interface

Exterior
– Roof of cooling chamber western red cedar 1x6 lap board left to weather naturally

Interior
– Douglas fir ceilings, doors, benches, and cabinets all finished with Cabot oil

Windows/Doors
– Loewen Windows and Doors, finished with Cabot oil

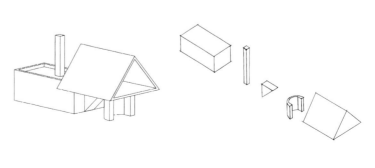

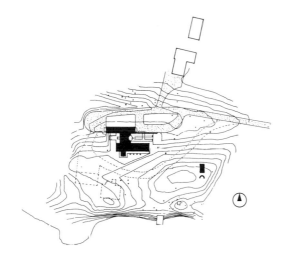

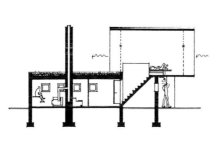
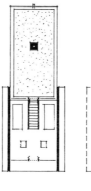

0   5   10ft.

CLIENT
Peter and Cynthia Emerson,
Duluth, Minnesota

ARCHITECT
Salmela Architect, Duluth, Minnesota

STRUCTURAL ENGINEER
Carroll Franck & Associates,
St. Paul, Minnesota

GENERAL CONTRACTOR
Rod & Sons Carpentry, Gilbert, Minnesota

LANDSCAPE ARCHITECT
Coen + Partners, Minneapolis, Minnesota

PHOTOS
Peter Bastianelli-Kerze, Eveleth, Minnesota

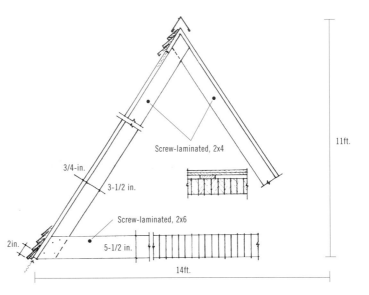

3/4-in.

3-1/2 in.

Screw-laminated, 2x4

Screw-laminated, 2x6

2in.

5-1/2 in.

11ft.

14ft.

Section, cooling room

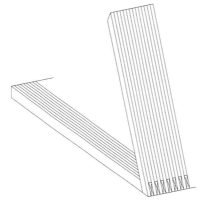

Corner detail, cooling room
[courtesy Carroll Franck & Associates]

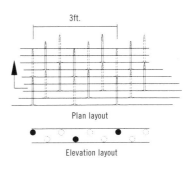

3ft.

Plan layout

Elevation layout

Screw schedule for laminations
[courtesy Carroll Franck & Associates]

Messenger House II

BRIAN MACKAY-LYONS ARCHITECT LIMITED

The year-round retirement home can accommodate visits by the clients' two daughters and their families. The house has numerous views of sea and land from a ridge that runs perpendicular to the southwest axis of Nova Scotia's south shore. The monolithic wedge-shaped form complements the scope of the ridge.

The program consists of a main house and a guest house separated by a covered court. One approaches the house from the minimalist east facade where the covered court gives access to the house and then opens up to frame a panoramic southeast view.

The plan makes clear distinction between what Louis Kahn calls "served" and "servant" spaces. The servant spaces [entry, pantry, stair, kitchen, baths, storage, workshop] occupy the northeast side, while the served spaces occupy the southwest side. A seven-bay "great room", consisting of main house living and dining, exterior court, and guest house living, is completely glazed on the ground floor. Plywood shear walls, painted cobalt blue, appear as giant book ends at either end of the great room. Three private sleeping places are located behind the shear walls.

A maple and slate clad totemic island separates served and servant spaces and gives focus to the interior. The protective servant zone offers a sense of "refuge," while the served zone offers "prospect". The geometries of the plan, section, and elevation are identical.

The project represents an ongoing search for the quality of "plainness" found in local vernacular platform frame construction and forms of sheds and barns. To this end, the 2x6 framed envelope of the house is clad in eastern white cedar shingles, corrugated Galvalume roof, and aluminum windows – all detailed to produce a taut-skinned effect.

A central spine of exposed 2x6 framing runs the length of the interior. A combination of plywood shear walls, let-in wood bracing, and horizontal steel pipes resolve the transverse wind loads.

Maple plywood panels, built ins and millwork fill the servant zone, study loft, and master bedroom giving the house warmth and human scale. Sliding cedar doors along the southwest facade help prevent heat loss in winter, and heat gain in summer.

While the house employs local material traditions, it exhibits a modernist aesthetic. This critical regionalist approach to design, as defined by historian Kenneth Frampton, expresses the optimism of a progressive view of Canadian Maritime culture.

Jury – A memorable form, the house has a contemporary design well conceived in the spirit of both the landscape and the traditional indigenous buildings. Simply detailed in wood for economy, the house is stretched lengthwise to provide commanding ocean views.

Product Specs

Frame
– Platform frame with 1/2-in. plywood and tongue and groove board sheathing, HSS horizontal pipe bracing, floor and ceiling joists of 2x10 with 5/8-in. plywood sheathing

Exterior
– Eastern white cedar shingles, No.2 grade 4in. exposure to weather naturally, outdoor decks finished with Lifetime stain by Valhalla Wood Preservatives Ltd.

Interior
– Maple plywood millwork and cabinets with solid 3/16-in. maple on exposed plywood edges in the servant zone, study loft, and master bedroom, tongue and groove1x6 spruce flooring in loft, painted drywall, first floor concrete topping 2in. with radiant heating; cabinets by D.W. Customized Kitchen Cabinets, Lunenburg, Nova Scotia

Windows/doors
– Clear anodized aluminum windows and doors, South Shore Glass Ltd., Bridgewater, Nova Scotia

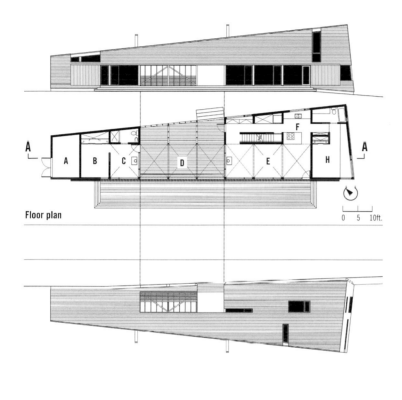

Floor plan

0 5 10ft.

Section A-A

A	Shed	E	Great room
B	Guest bedroom	F	Kitchen
C	Guest living	G	Loft/Guest bedroom
D	Courtyard	H	Master bedroom

CLIENT
The Messengers, Halifax, Nova Scotia

ARCHITECT
Brian MacKay-Lyons Architect Limited,
Halifax, Nova Scotia [Project team: Brian
MacKay-Lyons, Peter Blackie, Trevor
Davies, Chad Jamieson and Geoff Miller]

STRUCTURAL ENGINEER
Campbell Comeau Engineering Ltd.,
Halifax, Nova Scotia

GENERAL CONTRACTOR
Gordon MacLean, Dartmouth, Nova Scotia

PHOTOS
James Steeves, Atlantic Stock Images Inc.,
Seabright, NS

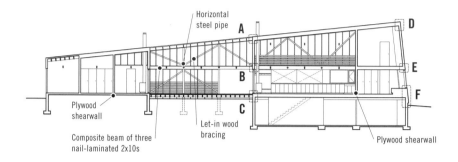

Horizontal
steel pipe

A

B

C

D

E

F

Plywood
shearwall

Composite beam of three
nail-laminated 2x10s

Let-in wood
bracing

Plywood shearwall

Detail A

Roof assembly:
- Corrugated steel roof
- Ice and water shield
- Plywood sheathing, 5/8-in.
- Strapping 2x3 on edge
  for ventilation
- Joists, 2x10 at 16in. o.c.
- Batt insulation, R30
- Poly vapor barrier, 6 mil
- Strapping 1x4 at 16in. o.c.
- Drywall, 1/2-in.

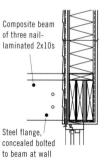

Corrugated
plastic roof

Minimum
overlap, 6in.

Cedar blocking
1 x 1-1/2

Roll vent

Detail B

Wall assembly:
- Eastern white cedar
  shingles, No.2 grade
  4in. exposure
- Building paper, 15lb.,
  taped and sealed at all
  openings
- Plywood sheathing,
  1/2-in.
- Studs, 2x6 @ 16in. o.c.

Composite beam
of three nail-
laminated 2x10s

Steel flange,
concealed bolted
to beam at wall

Detail C

Floor assembly:
- Concrete topping, 2in.
  with radiant heating
- Plywood subfloor, 5/8-in.
- Joists, 2x10 @ 16in. o.c.
- Batt insulation, R30
- Poly vapor barrier, 6 mil
- Strapping, 1x4 @ 16in. o.c.

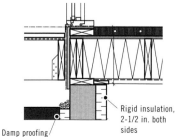

Damp proofing

Rigid insulation,
2-1/2 in. both
sides

Detail D

Roof assembly
as per Detail A

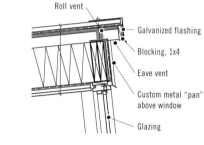

Roll vent

Galvanized flashing

Blocking, 1x4

Eave vent

Custom metal "pan"
above window

Glazing

Detail E

Floor assembly:
- Tongue and groove
  boards
- Joists, 2x10 @ 16in. o.c.
- Batt insulation, R30
- Strapping, 1x4 @
  16in. o.c.
- Drywall, 1/2-in.

Glazing

Detail F

Wall assembly:
- Eastern white cedar
  shingles, No.2 grade 4in.
  exposure
- Building paper, 15lb., taped
  and sealed at all openings
- Plywood sheathing, 1/2-in.
- Studs, 2x6 @ 16in. o.c.
- Batt insulation, R20
- Poly vapor barrier, 6 mil
- Drywall, 1/2-in.

Rigid
insulation,
2-1/2 in.

Outdoor Classrooms

MARPILLERO POLLAK ARCHITECTS

The outdoor classroom pavilions at Eib's Pond Park, Staten Island and Roy Wilkins Park, Southern Queens, New York offer outdoor venues for local children. The pavilions emphasize openness and durability, but also stand as advocates for the new educational purpose of their respective sites.

The AmeriCorps volunteers who built the structures had no experience reading construction documents, thus the construction process required the aid of a large framing model, field sketches, field verification, program adjustments and even homework assignments. During site visits, the architects demonstrated carpentry techniques required for the next phase of construction. One AmeriCorps member eventually became the crew leader for the classroom at Roy Wilkins Park.

Wood solved the structural and decorative problems of integrating man-made structures into a fragile, natural ecology. Moreover, the ready availability of stock sizes, ease of handling and forgiving nature of the material, helped beginning young carpenters to acquire building skills.

The Eib's classroom has its back to the approaching user, and looks outward to the pond. Variations in the spacing and pattern of framing members create a sense of lightness and filtered light that makes the perception of the interior more intense as one enters.

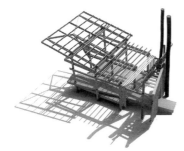

The classroom at Roy Wilkins Park uses the same module and materials but responds to a woodland rather than to water. As at the Eib pavilion, the entrance is a ramp that rises up as the ground drops away, but at the end of the Wilkins ramp one arrives at the precinct of birds, trees and leaves. Here, the opening up of the volume includes the roof that accommodates the trunk of a mature oak tree rising through the fretwork. Variations in height, pitch and transparency render the modulated roofline as a kind of formalized canopy. Light passing through the roof has a dappled effect as on a forest floor.

The architecture of the pavilions functions as an organizing element to help children and others situate themselves within the natural and urban environments that affect their day to day lives.

Jury – Small interventions affecting a large area, the outdoor classrooms expand the constituency of the park by providing access to a wetland while also protecting it. The exuberance, energy and robust exaggeration of the framed pavilions animate the landscape.

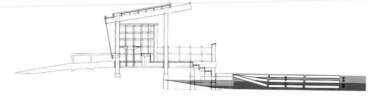

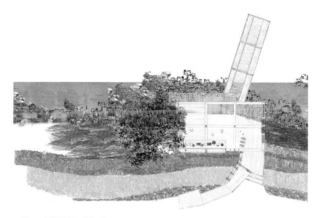

Plan, pavilion at Eib's Pond Park

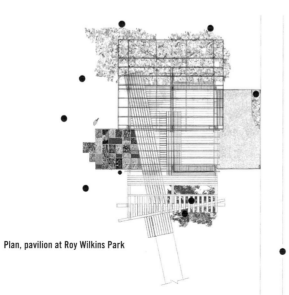

Plan, pavilion at Roy Wilkins Park

Product Specs

Frame
— Redwood framing from sustainably
managed forests in sizes: 2x12 joists,
3x8 ledgers for attaching to concrete
footings and ganged as columns, 3x12
main beams, and 2x8 miscellaneous
structures, including display shelves,
benches, table, entry screen and ramp
edges; plastic lumber for some vertical
and horizontal slats.

Exterior
Clear, corrugated pvc roof panels

CLIENT
New Yorkers for Parks, New York, New York

ARCHITECT
Marpillero Pollak Architects,
New York, New York

GENERAL CONTRACTOR
AmeriCorps Volunteers,
New York, New York

LANDSCAPE ARCHITECT
Marpillero Pollak Architects,
New York, New York

PHOTOS
Mark LaRocca, New York, New York

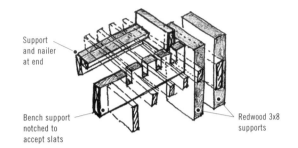

Support
and nailer
at end

Bench support
notched to
accept slats

Redwood 3x8
supports

Bench detail

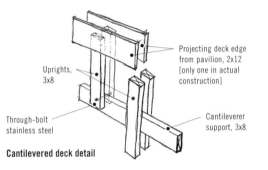

Projecting deck edge
from pavilion, 2x12
[only one in actual
construction]

Uprights,
3x8

Through-bolt
stainless steel

Cantileverer
support, 3x8

Cantilevered deck detail

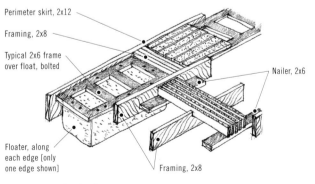

Perimeter skirt, 2x12

Framing, 2x8

Typical 2x6 frame
over float, bolted

Nailer, 2x6

Floater, along
each edge [only
one edge shown]

Framing, 2x8

Floating dock edge detail

Milanville House

BONE/LEVINE ARCHITECTS

Originally built as a barn about 1850 and known to have been a station on the Underground Railroad, the weekend house is located at the base of a mountain overlooking the Delaware River in Milanville, Pennsylvania.

The desire to preserve the integrity of the post and beam barn, the elegantly proportioned interior, and the spirit of the place, led to its reincarnation as a one-room house. The salvageable components of the barn including the post and beam timber structure and roof, barn board siding, and bluestone foundation walls were incorporated into the design of the new building.

The original barn was supported on timber cribs until a new foundation was constructed consisting of a concrete wall at the fully backfilled west wall, and stud walls on stepped footings elsewhere where backfill is minimal. The new foundation, clad with the original bluestone, extends beyond the perimeter of the original structure thus allowing the timber structure to maintain an independent identity within the new house. The north, south and west walls are insulated 2x6 wood stud curtain walls.

The post and beam structure continues to support the roof and two sleeping lofts as well as the river-facing, east facade where an operable wall of glass doors, wood shutters, insect screens and wooden blinds hang from tracks. The wall is operable across the length of the facade for an adaptable interface between interior and exterior.

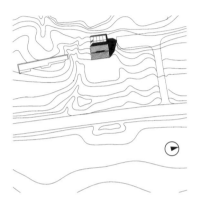

Only one timber cross beam was replaced, however, the roof is reinforced by hollow steel Y-braces supporting steel I-beam purlins at the mid-span of the log rafters. Inserted steel tension cables improve the lateral resistance of the timber frames.

The project is designed as a single, large cabinet. Beyond the exposed timbers, the interior floors are finished with cherry, and all cabinets cleanly detailed with maple-veneer plywood. Windows on the gable ends are "outboard" of the wall so that when opened one sees an unadorned punched opening from the inside.

The original barn board siding that allowed sliver-rays of light into the interior were reused as sliding shutters in front of the glass for lighting control, privacy, protection from the elements, and memory.

Jury – With re-used exterior siding over the original timber frame, and by retaining its position on the site, the barn is as a ghost of its former life. The exterior detail is exquisite with windows pushing through the facade, and with vertical spaces between board siding on sliding doors allowing penetration of light.

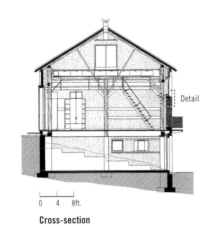

Cross-section

0　4　8ft.

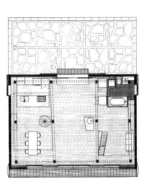

Plan

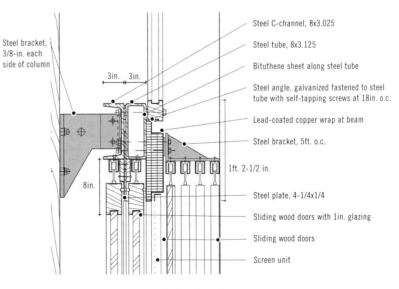

Detail

Steel bracket,
3/8-in. each
side of column

3in.　3in.

8in.

Steel C-channel, 8x3.025

Steel tube, 8x3.125

Bituthene sheet along steel tube

Steel angle, galvanized fastened to steel
tube with self-tapping screws at 18in. o.c.

Lead-coated copper wrap at beam

Steel bracket, 5ft. o.c.

1ft. 2-1/2 in.

Steel plate, 4-1/4x1/4

Sliding wood doors with 1in. glazing

Sliding wood doors

Screen unit

Detail: East wall, connection of track assembly to timber column

Product Specs

Frame
– Timber frame with re-use of original timbers and some new timbers with insulated, painted drywall 2x6 stud walls as exterior curtain walls; original log rafters and wood deck boards braced by a new steel purlin system; lead-coated copper standing seam on rigid insulation board over 3/4-in. plywood sheathing and original roof boards; floor joists 2x10 for main floor and lofts

Exterior
– Stained shiplap western red cedar siding finished with grey-pigmented boiled linseed oil by Wilbur + Williams
– High performance Coatings / California Paints, Storm Stain

Interior
– Painted drywall finish with some cement board panels; cherry flooring and maple veneer plywood cabinets finished with clear lacquer by Chemtec: Opticlear 900

Windows/doors
– Custom made in recycled yellow pine by the building contractor

Wall construction

Corrugated LCC siding, 3/4-in.
Plywood, 3/4-in.
Stud, 2x6
Cement board, 3/8-in.
Interior finish

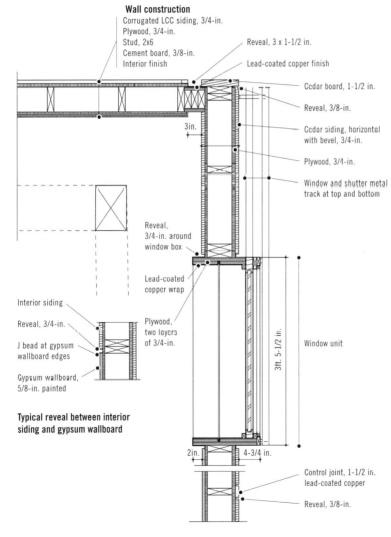

Reveal, 3 x 1-1/2 in.

Lead-coated copper finish

Cedar board, 1-1/2 in.

Reveal, 3/8-in.

Cedar siding, horizontal
with bevel, 3/4-in.

Plywood, 3/4-in.

Window and shutter metal
track at top and bottom

3in.

Reveal,
3/4-in. around
window box

Lead-coated
copper wrap

Plywood,
two layers
of 3/4-in.

3ft. 5-1/2 in.

Window unit

Interior siding

Reveal, 3/4-in.

J bead at gypsum
wallboard edges

Gypsum wallboard,
5/8-in. painted

**Typical reveal between interior
siding and gypsum wallboard**

2in.   4-3/4 in.

Control joint, 1-1/2 in.
lead-coated copper

Reveal, 3/8-in.

**Plan of pushed window
and corner framing**

CLIENT
Jane Cyphers

ARCHITECT
Joe Levine, R.A, Bone/Levine Architects,
New York, New York [Project team: Barbara
Wronska-Kucy, Koon Wee, Paul Deppe]

STRUCTURAL ENGINEER
Edy Zingher, ETNA Consulting,
New York, New York

GENERAL CONTRACTOR
Larry Braverman,
Beach Lake, Pennsylvania

PHOTOS
Jacek M. Kucy, New York, New York,
jmk@jmk-gallery.com

The Ocean Education Center in Dana Point, California realizes the long-held dream of the Ocean Institute to establish an education and research facility. Its marine labs, aquarium exhibits, classrooms, multi-purpose auditorium, and sea animal life support systems encourage public education, appreciation and protection of the ocean and marine life.

The Ocean Education Center seeks to evoke the California marine laboratories of Laguna Beach, and Monterey Bay, small complexes of wood framed one- and two-story buildings built of native materials and reflecting the rugged character of the marine environment. Thus the Center uses exposed post and beam of Alaskan yellow cedar glulam construction infilled with lumber and steel framing.

Rather than a single, imposing, large-scale structure, the Center is an ensemble of six one- and two-story buildings that observe the scale and massing of coastal architecture. The small-scale buildings with their random roof elevations preserve the views from the scenic Dana Point headlands and harbor. The use of western red cedar siding, no-glare metal and non-reflective glass blend the facility into the natural coastal landscape. The cedar siding is detailed as a ventilated rain shield to encourage drying and discourage the formation of mildew and mold.

The traditional forms and scales of the buildings optimize the relationship to the sun and wind of the California coast. Use of gable and shed roofs, and careful orientation of the buildings affords opportunities for natural ventilation, day lighting of interior spaces and solar control.

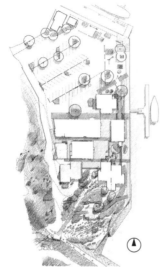

Natural materials such as Douglas fir, Western red and Alaskan yellow cedar stand up well to the often harsh, coastal environment. Birch boards and panels provide warm, durable interior finishes.

Jury – The considered composition of buildings has the loose randomness of a fishing village, and genuinely appears as a series of accretions built over time. The scale and choice of wood materials are appropriate to the coastal environment.

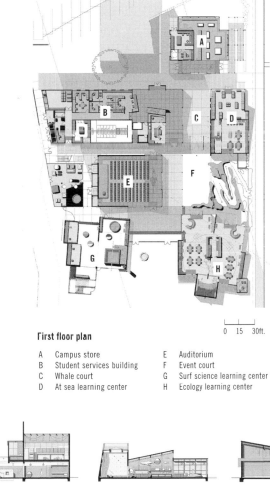

First floor plan

A   Campus store
B   Student services building
C   Whale court
D   At sea learning center
E   Auditorium
F   Event court
G   Surf science learning center
H   Ecology learning center

0   15   30ft.

Surf science learning center

Ecology learning center

Auditorium

Product Specs

Frame
– Exposed post and beam Alaskan yellow cedar glulam with columns of 6x6 to 12x12, and beams of 4x8 to 6-1/8 in. x 12, wood and steel infill framing, Douglas fir tongue and groove decking over roof beams, R30 rigid insulation and 1/2-in. exterior plywood facing, standing seam metal roof, radiant-heated floor slab; custom steel connectors where exposed, concealed steel connectors by Simpson
– Glulam supplier: Felmar Framing/Ganahl Lumber

Exterior
– Western red cedar 1x6 siding finished with Olympic Stain, semi-transparent, penetrating, oil-based stain; exposed timber structure finished with Olympic Stain, transparent, penetrating, oil-based sealer

Interior
– Painted gypsum board and birch plywood finished with clear catalyzed lacquer, medium density fiberboard with solid surface tops; plumbing fixtures by Kohler and Elkay

Windows/Doors
– Aluminum store-front windows, western red cedar custom doors by Turi Doors, overhead roll-up doors by Cookson Doors

CLIENT
Ocean Institute, Dana Point, California

ARCHITECT
Bauer and Wiley Architects,
Newport Beach, California

STRUCTURAL ENGINEER
Johnson & Nielsen Associates,
Irvine, California

GENERAL CONTRACTOR
MATT Construction,
Santa Fe Springs, California

LANDSCAPE ARCHITECT
Spurlock Poirier Landscape Architects,
San Diego, California

PHOTOS
Tom Bonner Photography and RMA
Photography, Venice and Tustin, California

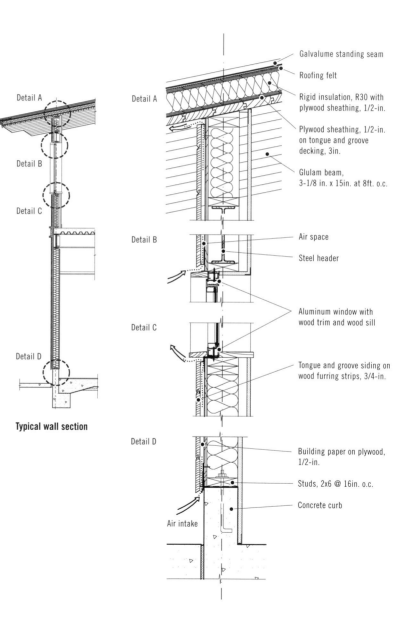

Detail A

Detail B

Detail C

Detail D

Typical wall section

Detail A

Galvalume standing seam

Roofing felt

Rigid insulation, R30 with
plywood sheathing, 1/2-in.

Plywood sheathing, 1/2-in.
on tongue and groove
decking, 3in.

Glulam beam,
3-1/8 in. x 15in. at 8ft. o.c.

Detail B

Air space

Steel header

Aluminum window with
wood trim and wood sill

Detail C

Tongue and groove siding on
wood furring strips, 3/4-in.

Detail D

Building paper on plywood,
1/2-in.

Studs, 2x6 @ 16in. o.c.

Concrete curb

Air intake

Bunch Residence

TURNBULL GRIFFIN HAESLOOP

Located in the hills above Napa, the 2,500sf house perches on a steeply sloped site. The driveway leads up from the valley below and swings around on the uphill side of the house to open onto a courtyard, the only level ground on the site, and formed by separate garages dug into the hill and by the tall wall of the house. Seating, water features and turnaround space for cars allow the courtyard to function as an outdoor entry room.

The wall of the house, clad with vertical 2x6 tongue and groove cedar boards left to weather naturally, bends with the shape of the hill and inflects for the front porch and door. Inside, the spaces seem to float from the tall wall to the view beyond. An updated version of a Japanese tokonoma separates the living spaces from the entry and creates a sense of drama by allowing the view to unfold as one enters the living area. A window wall opening out towards the trees and views stretches along the entire length of the house.

The roof holds the drama in contrast to the standard insulated 2x6 wall construction and painted drywall. Exposed 2x10 rafter framing of the ceiling folds and steps up at the center of the living room, allowing for the living room to project forward for dramatic views. It opens onto a cantilevered deck. A mature oak tree grows through the deck, offering shade and filtered light.

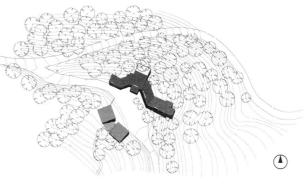

The master bedroom, at the southern end of the house, is entered through an elegant Chinese red door and features a Japanese cedar soaking tub. The large tub is set into an alcove framed by Douglas fir posts and windows that open out to the trees and valley.

Interior treatments include exposed Douglas fir tongue and groove 1x4 decking, vertical grain Douglas fir plywood cabinets, and cherry floors finished with clear varnish.

Jury – The design makes a relaxed, informal gesture in the landscape and cleverly shapes an entry courtyard. Detailed with skill in an open flowing plan, the house interior uses wood with subtle and unpronounced influence.

Product Specs

Frame
– Platform construction of 2x6 framing and exposed 2x10 Douglas fir rafters, exposed Douglas fir tongue and 1x4 decking; outdoor redwood deck

Exterior
– Western red cedar vertical 1x6 tongue and groove siding left to weather naturally

Interior
– Painted gypsum board, cherry flooring and vertical grain Douglas fir plywood cabinets finished with clear satin polyurethane

Windows/Doors
– Lincoln windows and doors

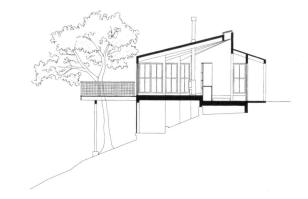

Section A-A

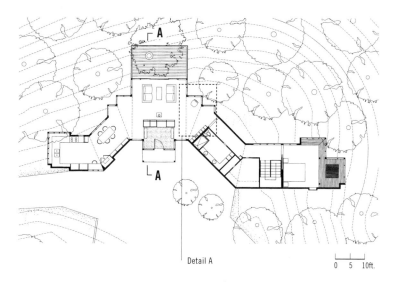

Detail A

0   5   10ft.

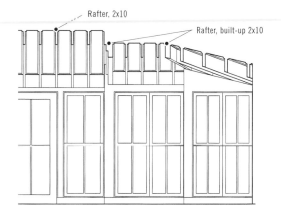

Detail A: Section through rafter framing

Rafter, 2x10

Rafter, built-up 2x10

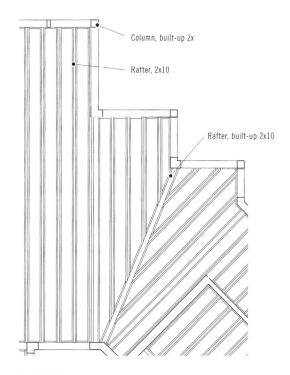

Column, built-up 2x

Rafter, 2x10

Rafter, built-up 2x10

Detail A: Rafter framing plan

CLIENT
M. Caldwell and C. Bunch

ARCHITECT
Turnbull Griffin Haesloop, Berkeley,
California

STRUCTURAL ENGINEER
The Hartwell Company, Sebastopol,
California

GENERAL CONTRACTOR
Sawyer Construction, Sebastopol, California

LANDSCAPE ARCHITECT
Lutsko Associates, San Francisco, California

PHOTOS
Matthew Millman Photography,
El Cerrito, California

The structure is cedar 6x6 post and beam with the upper level using 2x6 stud construction. Horizontal cedar siding on the upper level picks up on the open horizontal slats of the lower level. Exterior surfaces are stained with Cabot bleaching oil for an even, weathered finish. The telescope is supported on an independent concrete column, so as not to be affected by movement and deflection of the lighter wood structure.

The structure is unheated as temperature variations obscure star gazing, thus wood provides good insulating characteristics, and doesn't sweat like metals nor retain moisture as masonry might.

Product Specs

Frame
- Post and beam construction of 6x6 western red cedar, upper level walls of uninsulated 2x6 construction

Exterior
- Western red cedar horizontal 1x5 siding, and 1x5 slats finished with Cabot bleaching oil

Interior
- Maple veneer plywood cabinets and wall panels with horizontal maple battens, all finished with clear lacquer, ipe hardwood floors

Windows/Doors
- Custom made by contractor

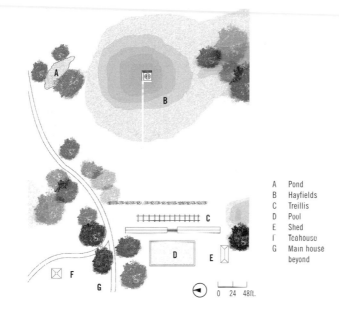

A Pond
B Hayfields
C Treillis
D Pool
E Shed
F Teahouse
G Main house
beyond

0 24 48ft.

Wood provided all of the sizes and shapes needed in the design, including slats, planks, sheathing, structural timber, millwork, and window frames. Precision carpentry achieves a simple volumetric look. The solid wood surfaces are flush at all edges including at the main doors. All corners are mitered on the exterior for a clean, sculptural presentation. The flexibility of the cedar siding makes a graceful transition from a flat to a curved surface on the west facade. The dimensions of the slats are coordinated with the stair riser for a totally integrated aesthetic.

Ipe, a sustainably harvested hardwood, is used in the floors for its extreme hardness and performance in harsh climates. The floor also serves as a structural diaphragm. The interior is sheathed in maple veneer plywood, with horizontal bands of solid maple. Maple is also used for the cabinetry and the desk.

Jury – The project takes the liberties of a traditional folly, however, its execution meets completely the specific program demands of an observatory. The wood details are clear and simple resulting in a lovely piece of sculpture.

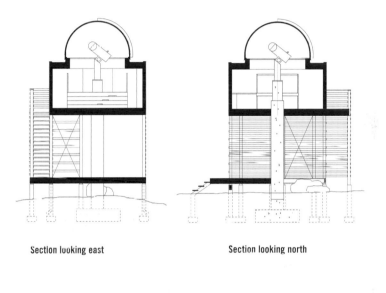

Section looking east

Section looking north

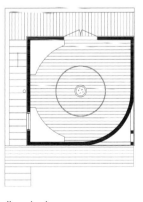

Upper level

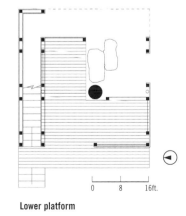

0   8   16ft.

Lower platform

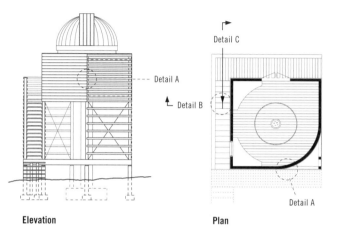

Elevation

Plan

Detail C

Detail A

Detail B

Detail A

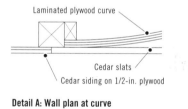

Laminated plywood curve

Cedar slats

Cedar siding on 1/2-in. plywood

Detail A: Wall plan at curve

Curve beyond

Curve beyond

Curve beyond

Cedar siding, 10in.

Cedar slats, 4in.

Detail A: Wall elevation at curve

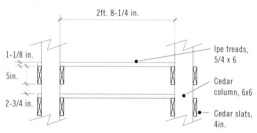

2ft. 8-1/4 in.

1-1/8 in.

5in.

2-3/4 in.

Ipe treads, 5/4 x 6

Cedar column, 6x6

Cedar slats, 4in.

Detail B: Stair tread section

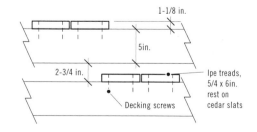

1-1/8 in.

5in.

2-3/4 in.

Decking screws

Ipe treads, 5/4 x 6in. rest on cedar slats

Detail C: Stair tread section

CLIENT
Dr. Jeffrey Ravetch, New York, New York

ARCHITECT
Wendy Evans Joseph Architecture,
New York, New York

GENERAL CONTRACTOR
Jim Romanchuk and Sons,
Stuyvesant, New York

PHOTOS
Wendy Evans Joseph Architecture,
New York, New York [p.95 top, p.98, p.99];
Pamela Cobb Photography, Berkeley,
California [p.93, p.96]; Albert Vecerka,
New York, New York [p.94]; Elliot Kaufman
Photography, New York, New York
[p.92, p.95 bottom]

Sitting high on a hill with a view of the Pacific Ocean, the surrounding homes range from California beach cottages of the 1930s to the modern, with no distinct architectural style.

Passive heating, natural ventilation and sustainable building materials were important. The addition is very much a glazed pavilion. Thus a 10ft. high x 15ft. wide wall of double 8mm translucent polycarbonate faces south for heat and light and privacy to the street, while the west and east elevations were stacked with low e-double glazed operable doors and windows for cross ventilation, light and connection to the site.

The structural system is a simple post and beam construction of 4x10 Douglas fir beams and 4x4 columns, assembled with hidden steel 5/8-in. dia. pin connections. Wood framing consists of 2x8 floor joists and insulated 2x4 stud walls, including narrow sections of seismic-resistant Simpson Strong Walls, clad with 3/8-in. marine-grade plywood. Medium density fiber board [MDF] panels and plywood are used for selected areas inside.

Product Specs

Frame

– Post and beam construction of 4x10 Douglas fir beams and 4x4 columns, 2x8 floor joists and insulated 2x4 wall studs 16in. o.c. clad with 3/8-in. plywood, narrow sections of seismic-resistant Simpson Strong Walls; Man a War clear matte water-proof sealer over all marine ply panels

Exterior

– Marine plywood, polycarbonate panels 8mm, glazing

Interior

– Medium density fiberboard [MDF] and plywood panels, Bamboo flooring [distributed through Solana Beach Cut and Dry]

Windows/doors

– T.M. Cobb, finished with clear water-based stain by Man a War

New | Existing

0 1 2m

Floor plan A Living/dining
B Living
C Bedroom

The roof diaphragm consists of a R-19 insulated 2x4 grid faced with 4x8 marine plywood on both sides and finished with a three-ply membrane and a 4in. galvanized metal edge all-around. The roof diaphragm connects to 4x10 framing laid over a grid of 4x10 that runs north to south on 4ft. centers. The ceiling reveals the exposed underside of the roof, marine plywood finished with clear sealer. At the intersection of the original and new roofs, 2x4 rafter tails rest on a new 4x10 beam that spans from the kitchen to the bathroom wall.

The storage system of opaque white polycarbonate demarcates and illuminates the entry on the east elevation. During the evening, the south elevation of translucent polycarbonate panels returns the interior light to the exterior, illuminating the front yard to the street.

Jury – A small magical renovation and addition that is full of ideas. It is a joyful experiment in transparency, translucency and the overall quality of light.

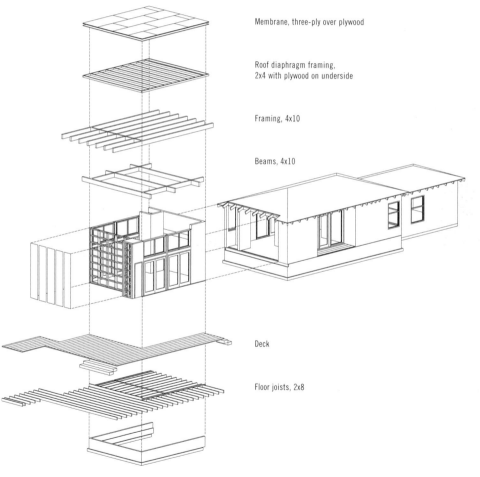

Membrane, three-ply over plywood

Roof diaphragm framing,
2x4 with plywood on underside

Framing, 4x10

Beams, 4x10

Deck

Floor joists, 2x8

CLIENT
The Lombardis, San Diego, California

ARCHITECT
Steven Lombardi, Architect, Dustin Davis,
San Diego, California

STRUCTURAL ENGINEER
John Nicita, Spring Valley, California

GENERAL CONTRACTOR
Steven Lombardi, Architect,
San Diego, California

PHOTOS
Tim Crowson [night photo], San Diego,
California and Steven Lombardi, Steven
Lombardi, Architect, San Diego
Drawings by Taylor Osborn

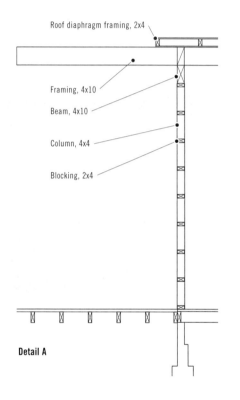

Roof diaphragm framing, 2x4

Framing, 4x10

Beam, 4x10

Column, 4x4

Blocking, 2x4

Detail A

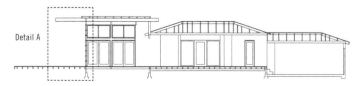

Detail A

Longitudinal section

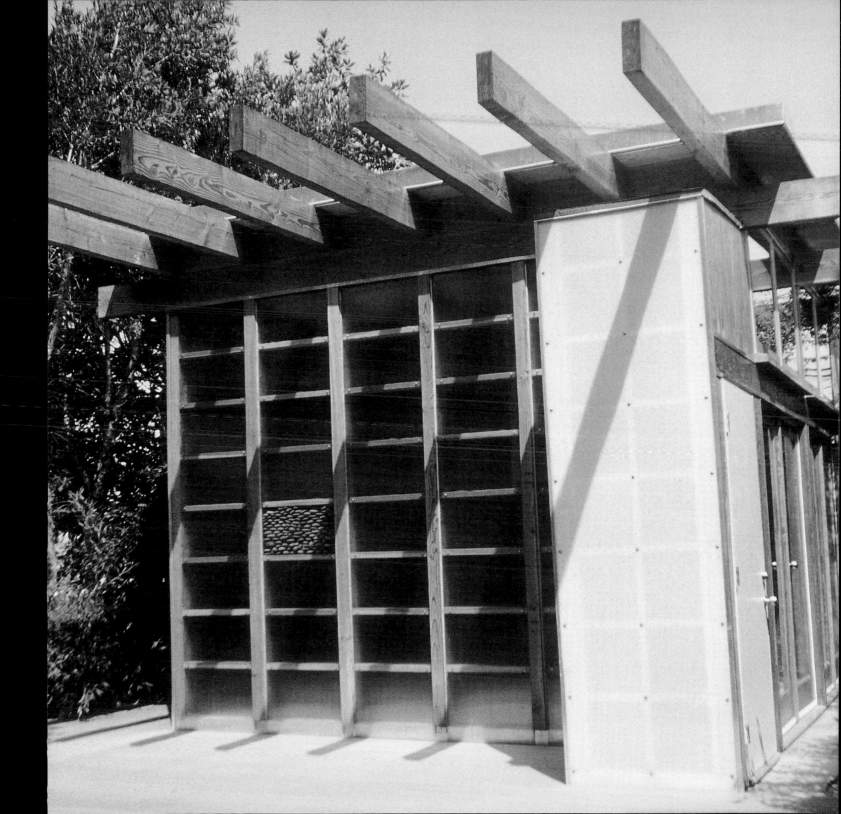

Bird Studies Canada Headquarters

MONTGOMERY SISAM ARCHITECTS INC.

The Bird Studies Canada headquarters houses Canada's leading non-profit conservation organization dedicated to advancing understanding, appreciation and conservation of wild birds and their habitats. The site on a former farm overlooking the inner bay of Lake Erie's Long Point Peninsula is a designated World Biosphere Reserve.

The project consolidates research and administrative facilities under one roof to support the organization's scientific goals and public education needs. The program demanded flexible workspaces, a library to house its wild bird database, meeting rooms and a lecture hall.

The design reflects the environmental ethos of the organization and provides a notable presence for the national institution. Two elemental wood-clad building forms create a backdrop to the existing farmhouse and courtyard: an events building of simple rectangular shape containing the lecture hall and kitchen, and an open office loft. A glazed entry connects both buildings and also acts as a gateway to the larger property and adjacent wetland, framing a view to Long Point. A stair tower projects from the loft wing and glows at night as a lantern in the courtyard.

Steel and wood make up a composite construction of steel post and beam with tongue and groove Douglas fir decking, 2x6 exterior and interior walls, and laminated strand lumber studs for the stair tower. Sandblasted and lacquered steel columns and beams allow the fir decking to stand out as dominant planes that are flat at the second floor, and gently sloping inward at the roof. In the support spaces, 2x8 wood ceiling joists spanning between the steel beams take lateral load from one direction, with the steel beams taking the load from the other direction.

d

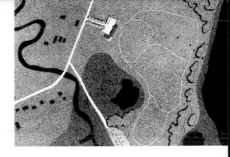

Wood was chosen in response to the environmental mandate of the institution and the numerous weathered barns and tobacco sheds of the area. Clad with factory-finished vertical shiplap wood siding, the buildings stand as strong forms on the landscape. The dark stain finish, however, has a muted effect in contrast to the warm tones of redwood color-stained horizontal 2x4 cedar used on a mechanical screen and the stair tower. The strong color contrast mimics that of birds with their dark wings and colored breasts.

Clear-lacquered maple veneer plywood furnishes the interior in modular work stations and suspended ceiling planes that conceal mechanical ducts, diffuse ceiling light and contrast elegantly with the fir decking and concrete floors.

Jury – The design takes a simple, elemental form and uses it to shape a significant outdoor space that also incorporates an existing house. The building has a spare composition and a modernist, taut wood skin that makes it a powerful symbol on the landscape.

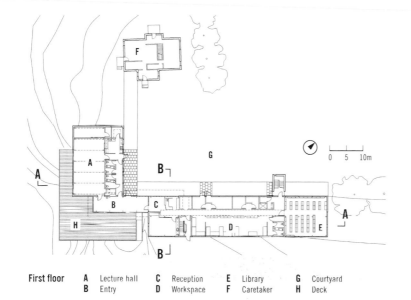

First floor
A Lecture hall C Reception E Library G Courtyard
B Entry   D Workspace F Caretaker H Deck

South elevation

West elevation

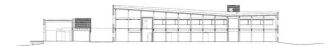

Section A-A

Section B-B

Product Specs

Frame

Steel post and beam, 2x8 ceiling joists between steel beams, tongue and groove Douglas fir decking, 3-1/2 x 5-1/4, moisture barrier, rigid insulation and modified bitumen roofing; curtain walls insulated 2x6, interior walls 2x6; floor-ceiling assembly and roof of 2x6 tongue and groove Douglas fir decking; laminated strand lumber [Timberstrand®] studs, 38mm x 286mm [approx. 2x12] to frame the stair tower

Exterior

– Factory-finished vertical V-joint 5/8-in. x 6 [16mm x 140mm] spruce wood siding by Maibec over horizontal strapping, horizontal 2x4 western red cedar on mechanical screen and the stair tower finished in redwood color-stain by Cabot Stain

Interior

– Painted drywall, concrete first floor, carpet second floor

Windows/doors

– Clear anodized aluminum windows and curtain wall, interior doors clear coat maple by Cambridge Doors

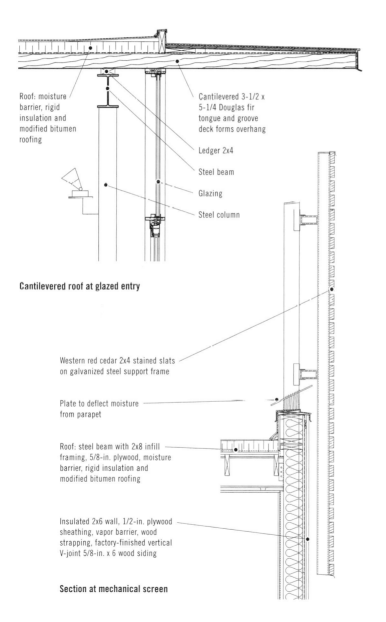

Roof: moisture barrier, rigid insulation and modified bitumen roofing

Cantilevered 3-1/2 x 5-1/4 Douglas fir tongue and groove deck forms overhang

Ledger 2x4

Steel beam

Glazing

Steel column

Cantilevered roof at glazed entry

Western red cedar 2x4 stained slats on galvanized steel support frame

Plate to deflect moisture from parapet

Roof: steel beam with 2x8 infill framing, 5/8-in. plywood, moisture barrier, rigid insulation and modified bitumen roofing

Insulated 2x6 wall, 1/2-in. plywood sheathing, vapor barrier, wood strapping, factory-finished vertical V-joint 5/8-in. x 6 wood siding

Section at mechanical screen

CLIENT
Bird Studies Canada, Port Rowan, Ontario

ARCHITECT
Montgomery Sisam Architects Inc., Toronto, Ontario

STRUCTURAL ENGINEER
Blackwell Engineering, Toronto, Ontario

GENERAL CONTRACTOR
Southside Construction, London, ON

PHOTOS
Steven Evans, Toronto, Ontario

separate garage with studio stands separately farther east.

The construction borrows from the tall timber corn cribs of the area. Glulam beams at 4ft. o.c. support the main floor and roof, and rest on painted steel columns at one end. The remainder consists of conventional wood framing of 2x6 studs, sawn joists and I-joists, with western cedar tongue and groove decking for second floor and 5/8-in. plywood roof sheathing.

Exterior siding is applied in both familiar and experimental ways. Rustic channel cedar siding rises to full height at the parent/guest wing to become a floating, open-jointed wall that screens a private entrance to the south. Vertical tongue and groove cedar clads much of the house but weaves together with the channel siding at a pivotal corner. Here, horizontal battens slip into the reveals of the channel siding and continue over the vertical cedar. Dark stain allows differences in texture, scale, and orientation to be perceived through light and shadow. Natural Douglas fir slats at the entry, loggia, and screened porch contrast with the dark stain.

Inside, channel siding in the parent/guest wing reduces the scale of the interior and provides a sense of separation and privacy. Birch plywood ceilings, perforated birch cabinets, cherry shelving and use of various stains provide moments of contrast.

Jury – The house is nicely resolved and appropriately recessive in a landscape that borders Lake Michigan where weather can be harsh. The exterior wood detailing has a northern European quality.

Product Specs

Frame
– Glulam beams 4x12 at 4ft. o.c., at second floor 3x10 Douglas fir timbers; infill framing with 2x6 studs. sawn joists and I-joists; second floor of western red cedar tongue and groove 2x6 decking, 5/8-in. plywood sheathing

Exterior
– Western red cedar rustic 1x8 channel siding, cedar tongue and groove 1x6 vertical siding; all finished with Cabot semi-transparent stain

Interior
– Western red cedar sanded rustic 1x8 channel siding finished with Cabot semi-transparent stain; smooth cedar tongue and groove 1x4 vertical siding on selected walls, birch veneer cabinets, cherry shelves all finished with Tung oil; Douglas fir flooring

Windows/doors
– Kolbe & Kolbe; Interior Doors: Simpson Fir Doors

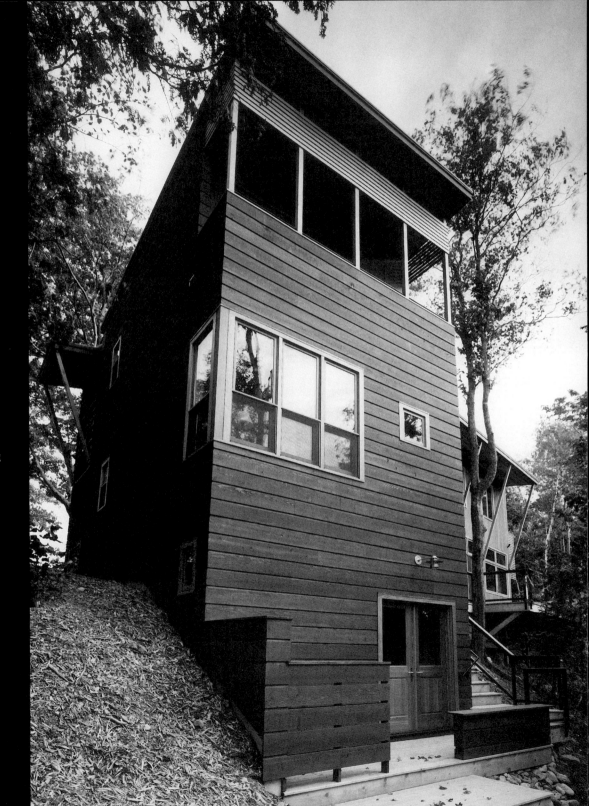

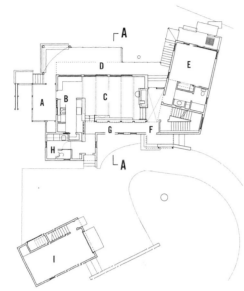

Main level plan

A	Screened porch
B	Kitchen
C	Living room
D	Deck
E	Guest bedroom
F	Entry
G	Hall
H	Laundry
I	Garage
J	Upper porch
K	Bedroom
L	Study
M	Guest bedroom
N	Loggia
O	Storage
P	Studio

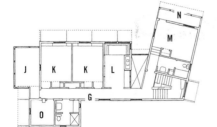

0 4 8ft

Upper level plan

Section A-A

CLIENT
Cornelius and Dorothy Alig

ARCHITECT
Betsy Williams, Ann Arbor, Michigan and
Cornelius Alig, Indianapolis, Indiana

STRUCTURAL ENGINEER
SDI, Ann Arbor, Michigan

GENERAL CONTRACTOR
David Webster Construction Inc.,
Traverse City, Michigan

PHOTOS
Peter Tata Architectural Photography,
Austin, Texas

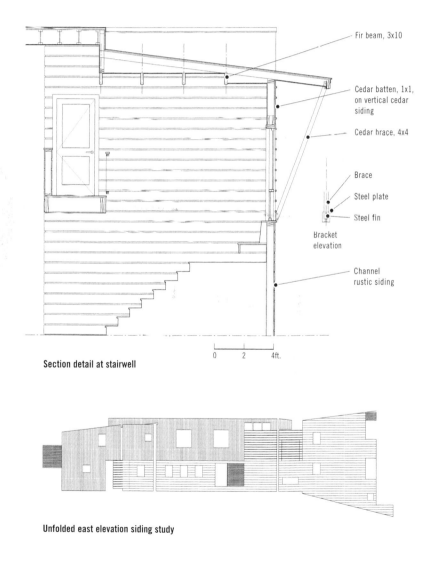

Fir beam, 3x10

Cedar batten, 1x1, on vertical cedar siding

Cedar hrace, 4x4

Brace

Steel plate

Steel fin

Bracket elevation

Channel rustic siding

0   2   4ft.

Section detail at stairwell

Unfolded east elevation siding study

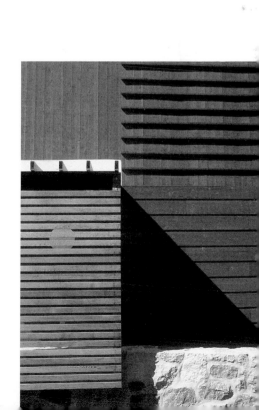

OTHER PUBLICATIONS BY TUNS PRESS

The Wood Design Awards 2002 : A North American Program of Architectural Excellence
ISBN 0-929112-49-0, 2002

Architecture Canada 2002 : The Governor General's Medals for Architecture
ISBN 0-929112-48-2, 2002

Barry Johns Architects : Selected Projects 1984-1998
ISBN 0-929112-32-6, 2000

Architecture Canada 1999 : The Governor General's Medals for Architecture
ISBN 0-929112-45-8, 2000

Brian MacKay-Lyons : Selected Projects 1986-1997
ISBN 0-929112-39-3, 1998

Works : The Architecture of A.J. Diamond, Donald Schmitt & Company, 1968-1995
ISBN 0-929112-31-8, 1996

Patkau Architects : Selected Projects 1983-1993
ISBN 0-929112-28-8, 1994

A Pictorial History of St. Paul's Anglican Church, Halifax, Nova Scotia
ISBN 0-929112-19-9, 1993

For additional information, please see our website at tunspress.dal.ca.

For the Wood Design Awards information and registration: www.WoodDesignAwards.com.